Light Makes a Rainbow

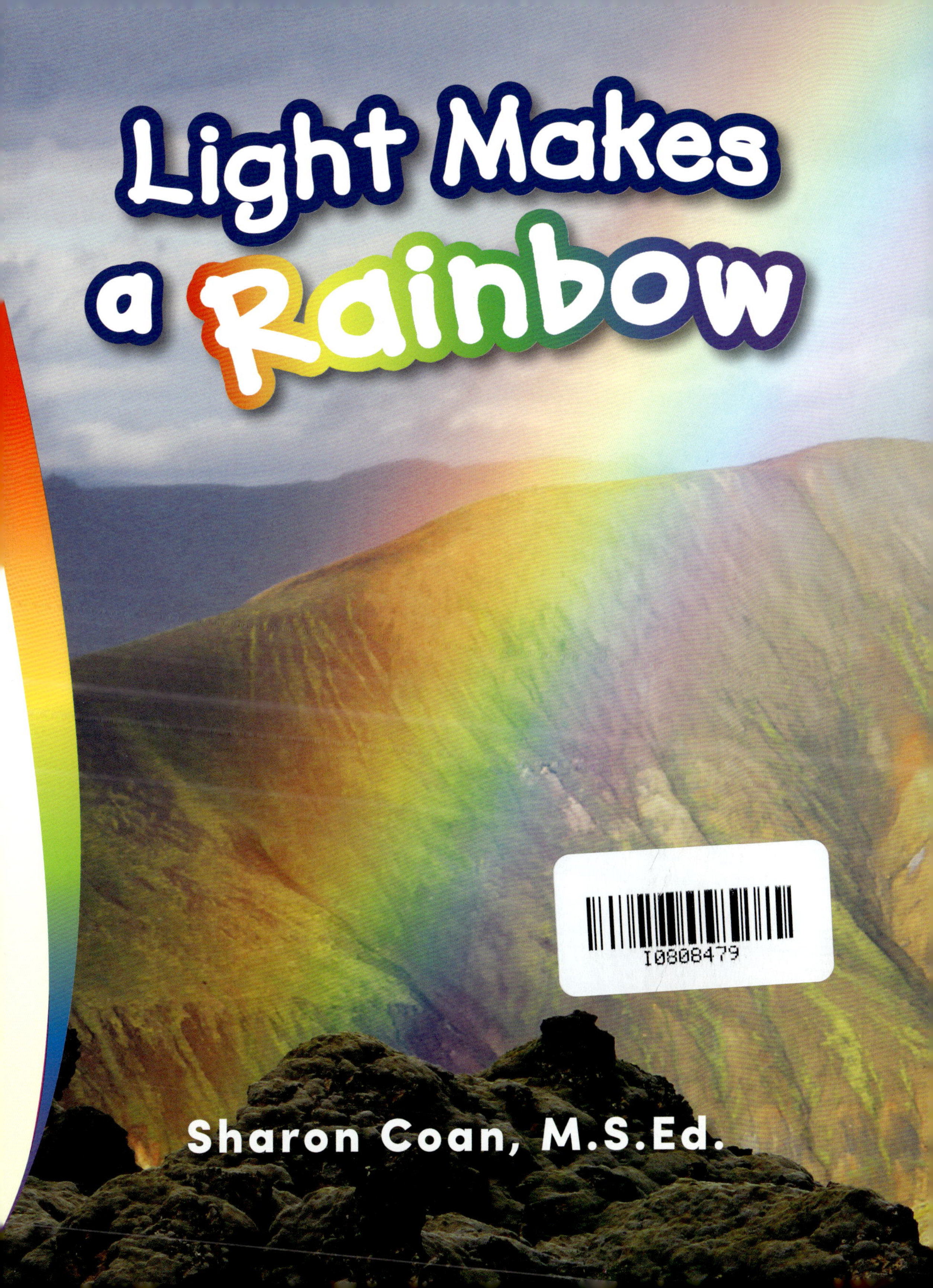

Sharon Coan, M.S.Ed.

Consultants

Sally Creel, Ed.D.
Curriculum Consultant

Leann Iacuone, M.A.T., NBCT, ATC
Riverside Unified School District

Jill Tobin
California Teacher of the Year
Semi-Finalist
Burbank Unified School District

Image Credits: pp.6–7, 16–17, 24 Andyworks/iStock; p.16 (top) Tim Bradley; pp.20–21 (illustrations) Janelle Bell-Martin; all other images from Shutterstock.

Library of Congress Cataloging-in-Publication Data

Coan, Sharon, author.
Light makes a rainbow / Sharon Coan, M.S.Ed.; consultants, Sally Creel, Ed.D. curriculum consultant, Leann Iacuone, M.A.T., NBCT, ATC Riverside Unified School District, Jill Tobin, California Teacher of the Year Semi-Finalist Burbank Unified School District.
pages cm
Summary: "Light is very important. It helps us see. Sometimes, light makes a rainbow of different colors. Light is a kind of energy."— Provided by publisher.
Audience: K to grade 3.
Includes index.
ISBN 978-1-4807-4566-7 (pbk.)
ISBN 978-1-4807-5056-2 (ebook)
1. Light—Juvenile literature.
2. Color—Juvenile literature. I. Title.
QC360.C58 2015
535—dc23

2014013152

Teacher Created Materials
5301 Oceanus Drive
Huntington Beach, CA 92649-1030
http://www.tcmpub.com

ISBN 978-1-4807-4566-7

Table of Contents

Making a Rainbow

You see rain. You see the sun.

You know what that means. You see a rainbow!

A rainbow happens when light goes through water drops.

The drops bend the light. When the light bends, it splits into colors.

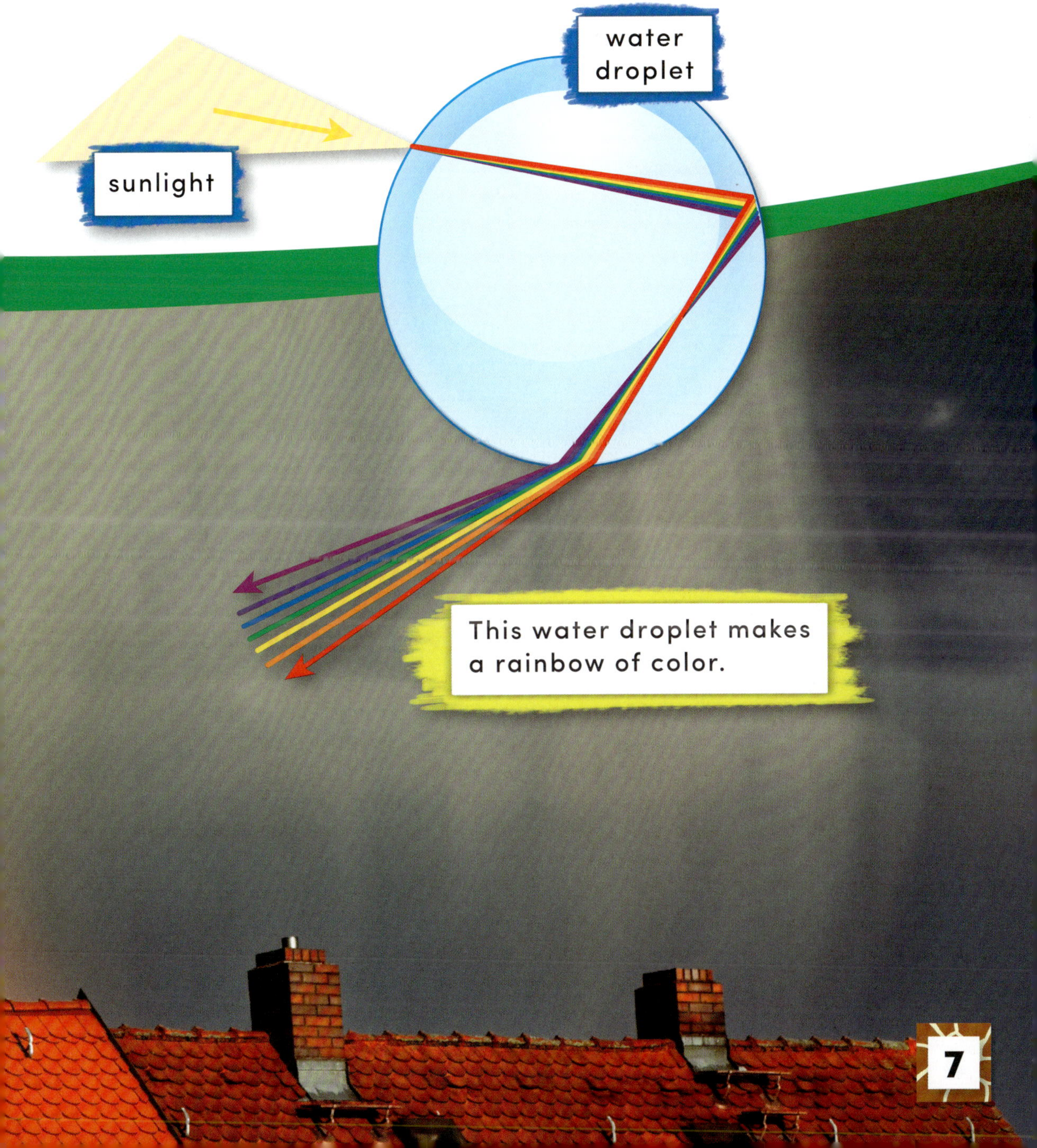

This water droplet makes a rainbow of color.

What Is Light?

Light is a kind of **energy**. It moves very fast.

Energy

Energy is the ability to do work or be active.

Scientists think light moves faster than all other things.

All of the things on this page give off light.

The energy of light is in small parts. The parts move together in waves.

Light waves move like ripples in a pond.

The waves are called **light waves**.

Light and Color

Light from the sun holds all the colors mixed together.

Sunlight looks white, but it has all the colors.

Each color has its own **wavelength.** A wavelength is how wide the wave is.

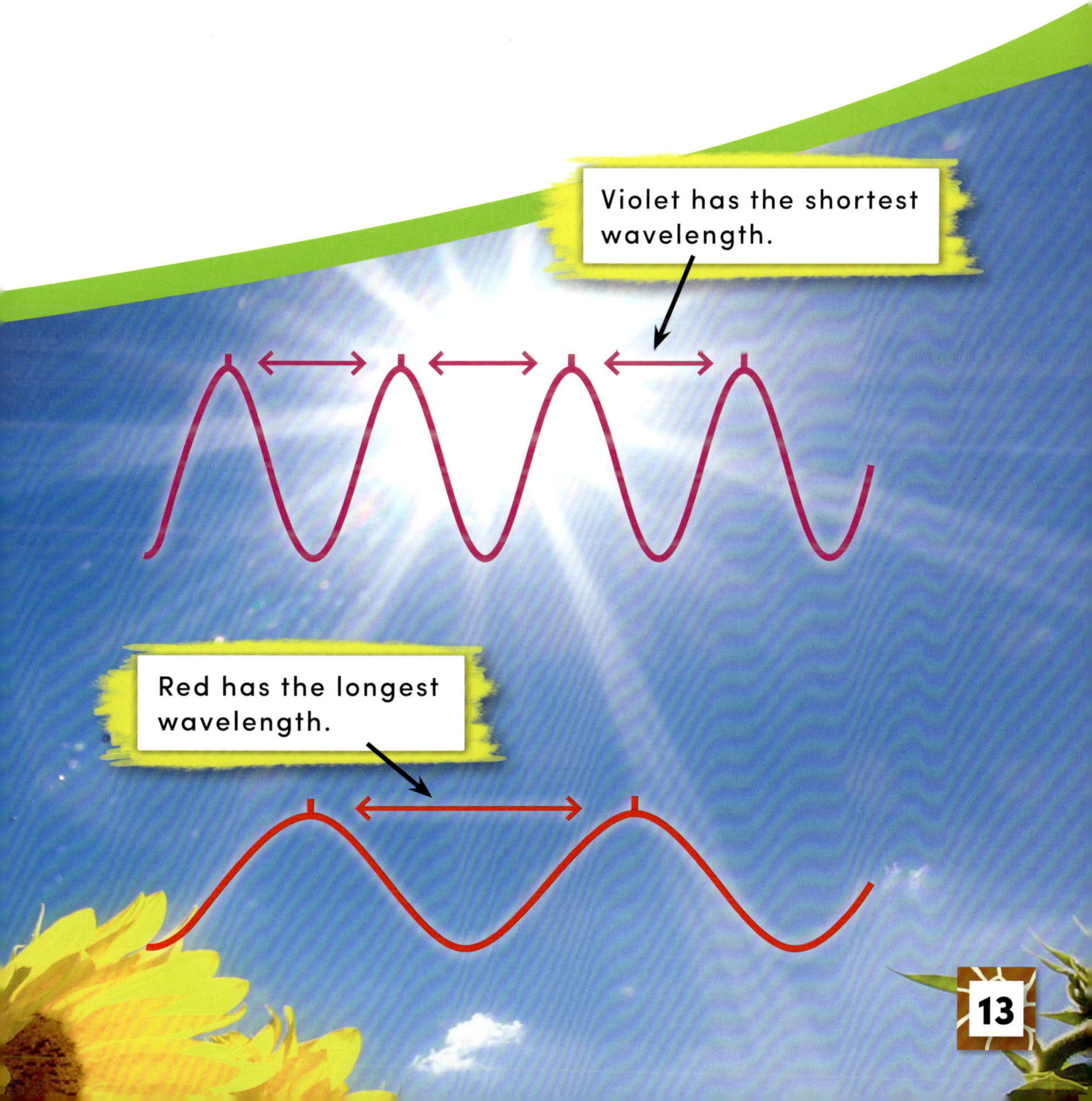

Drops of water can bend the waves of light. When they do, the color waves line up.

Water drops can bend light.

The colors line up from the longest wave to the shortest. They always line up in the same order.

Prisms can bend light, too!

Rainbow Colors

Think of a man named Roy G. Biv. The letters of his name stand for the colors!

The colors are red, orange, yellow, green, blue, indigo, and violet.

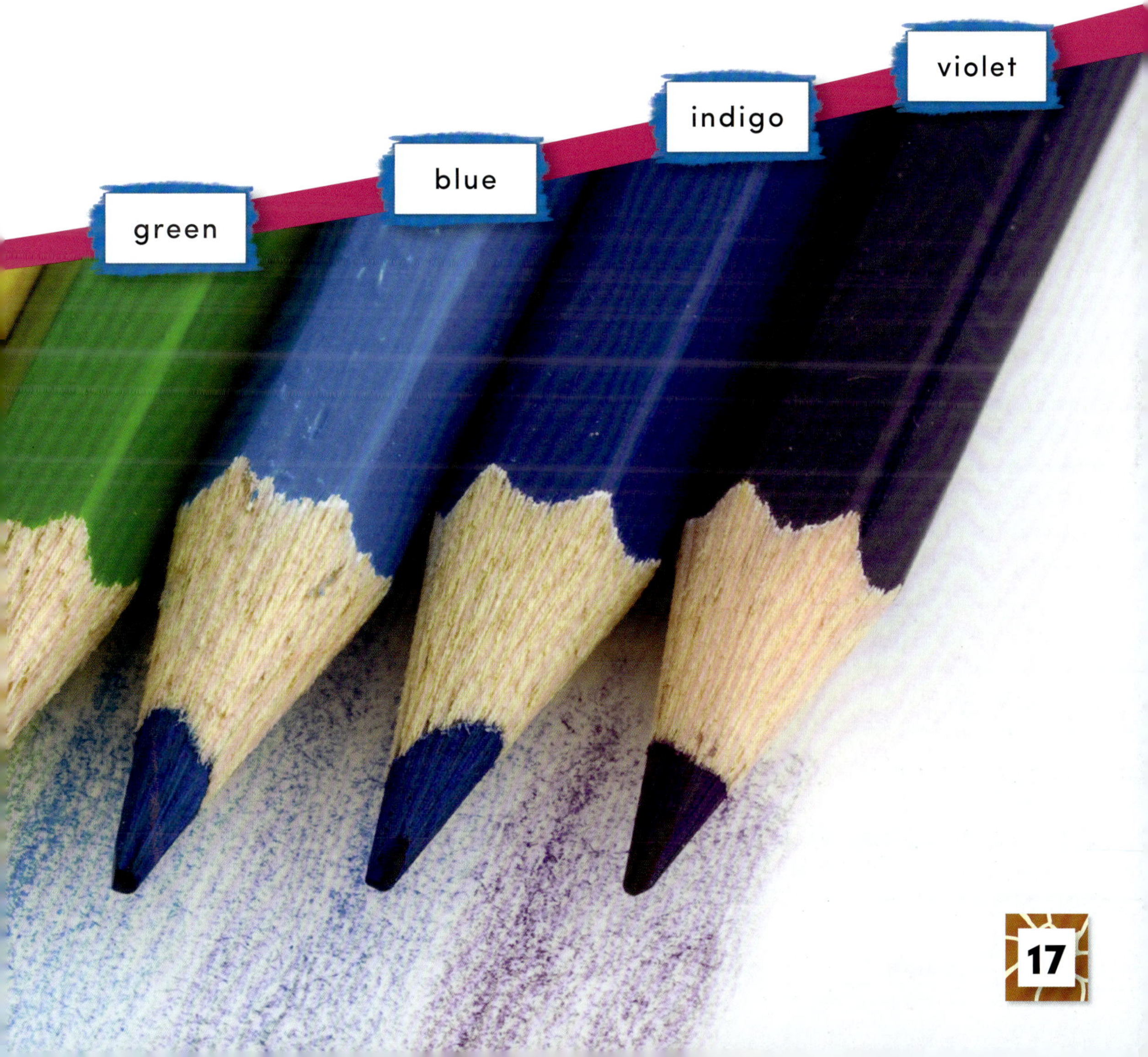

The colors come out when the sun shines through the rain. They make a pretty rainbow!

Let's Do Science!

What happens when light goes through water? Try this and see!

What to Get

- paper and pencil
- spray bottle

What to Do

1. Fill a spray bottle with water.

1

2. Go outside on a sunny day.

2

3. Hold your spray bottle in front of you. Quickly spray water into the air a few times.

3

4. What do you see? Draw what you observed on a sheet of paper.

4

Glossary

energy—usable power that comes from heat, electricity, or light

light waves—the way light flows in an up and down motion

scientists—people who study science

wavelength—the distance between the tops of two waves

Index

Your Turn!

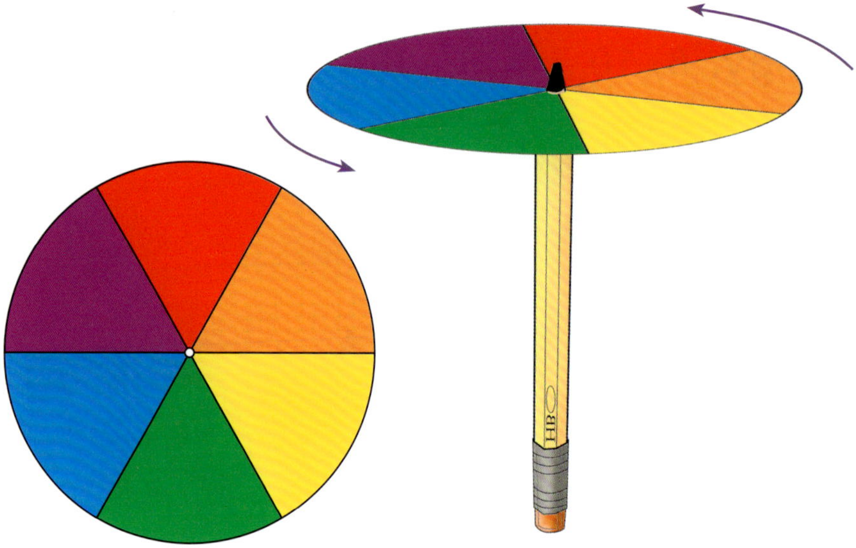

Spinning Colors

Cut a circle out of paper. Draw lines to make six sections. Color the sections to match the picture above. Hold a pencil on the middle of the circle and spin it quickly. What do you see?